ice cream

ice cream

Liz Franklin

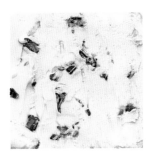

photography by William Lingwood

RYLAND
PETERS
& SMALL

LONDON NEW YORK

Commissioning Editor
Elsa Petersen-Schepelern

Editor Susan Stuck

Production Jacquie Horner

Art Director Gabriella Le Grazie

Publishing Director Alison Starling

Food Stylist Liz Franklin

Prop Stylist Chloe Brown

First published in USA in 2005
by Ryland Peters & Small, Inc.
519 Broadway, 5th Floor
New York, NY 10012
www.rylandpeters.com

10 9 8 7 6 5 4 3 2

ISBN-13: 978-1-84172-822-3
ISBN-10: 1-84172-822-5

Library of Congress
Cataloging-in-Publication Data

Franklin, Liz.
  Ice cream / Liz Franklin ; photography by
William Lingwood.
    p. cm.
  Includes index.
  ISBN 1-84172-822-5
  1. Ice cream, ices, etc. I. Title.
TX795.F75 2005
641.8'62–dc22
                              2004016024

Printed in China

For Michelle

NOTES

● All spoon measurements are level unless otherwise stated.

● Eggs are large unless otherwise specified. Uncooked or partly cooked
eggs should not be served to the very old, frail, young children,
pregnant women, or those with compromised immune systems.

Author's acknowledgments

With huge thanks to the wonderful team at RPS, Elsa in particular,
for asking me to write this book, so letting me indulge myself in the
guilt-free consumption of ice cream. To Paul, for the chuckles, the
encouragement, and the beautiful design that made this a book of
which I am very proud. Thanks too to William Lingwood, for his
patience and beautiful photography—and to Estelle for the giggles
and great lunches at the shoots! My thanks and my love also go out
to my dear and much-missed friend Michelle, who gave me my first
ever 'proper' ice cream machine all those years ago, and to my sons
Chris, Oli and Tim who keep me on my toes with their continuing
enthusiasm and appetite for homemade ice cream. Big hugs to my
mum and dad for magical ice cream memories and special thanks
to my many wonderful friends who tasted and tested along the way,
in particular Jan, Patricia, and Rosie—and to PJ too—for helping
with the words, when I sometimes couldn't find them.

contents

have fun freezing ...

I've always adored ice cream. As a small child, the tinkling chimes of the ice cream truck were the signal to run out to buy a cone topped with a whirl of light-as-air ice cream and chocolate jimmies.

Years passed, but my enthusiasm for ice cream continued. At college in the seaside town of Scarborough, hardly a day went by without a visit to the harbor-front ice cream parlor for a regular treat—two CD-size chocolate wafers sandwiching a flurry of white-as-snow ice cream.

My happy habit continued, until I bought an ice cream on a marina in Portugal. The cone was made from crisp waffled cookie and was almost the size of the Olympic torch. It would easily have outfaced me, had it not been filled with the most exquisite ice cream I had ever tasted. Not whipped and white this time, but dense, delicious, and the color of rich yellow cream. It was flecked with the tiny black seeds from plump Madagascan vanilla beans and each mouthful was pure bliss. This was real ice cream—and so began my ongoing love affair with homemade ice cream.

I started by making the easiest of all Italian ice creams, semifreddo, a meringue-like cloud of whipped egg whites folded into a delicious creamy base, which prevents the mixture from freezing completely solid. The result is a soft-scoop ice that doesn't need a machine. I was delighted with the results and thrilled with the compliments. Keen to try out other ice creams and sorbets, I invested in the most basic of electric ice cream machines—the kind where the bowl is stored in the freezer until just before churning.

Over the years, I have used several excellent machines and all of them have more than earned their keep. I am delighted that my current machine is restaurant-grade.

An ice cream can capture summer in a cone or add something special to a hot winter dessert. A sorbet or slush can solve the problem of something light and luscious to end a substantial meal. Simple or sophisticated, ices make a tempting treat for all ages.

Commercially made, chemically enhanced ice creams can never compare to those made at home with fresh, natural ingredients. Premium-grade commercial ice creams do contain better ingredients, but they are expensive to buy and flavors are limited.

So here I am, sharing my favorite frozen treasures, in the hope that you will love and use them every bit as much as I do.

Have fun freezing!

equipment

Electric ice cream machines

An electric ice cream machine is a blessing for people who make their own ice cream regularly. Your choice of machine will be influenced by the number of times it will be used—and cost. The most basic electric machine is made up of a main body housing a motor and paddle unit. A separate gel-filled inner bowl is placed in a freezer overnight, then removed and attached to the motor unit when the mixture is ready to be frozen. The disadvantage with this type of machine is that the inner bowl has to be refrozen after each batch of ice cream.

Spend five or six times this amount, and you can buy a machine with a built-in self-freezing unit. This type of machine will churn about a quart at a time and be capable of making further batches immediately.

Making ice cream by hand

You can also make good ice cream without a machine. It takes longer and requires more elbow grease, but you will still be rewarded for your efforts. The mixture should be frozen in a shallow container. When almost solid, beat it well with a wire whisk or electric beater until smooth, then return to the freezer. Repeat the process twice more to break down the ice crystals, and the result will be a smooth, silky ice cream.

After freezing, all ice creams should be stored in well-sealed, freezerproof containers to prevent freezer burn. Delicate ice creams will easily take up flavors from other foods stored nearby, so tight-fitting lids are important.

Homemade ice cream is best eaten as soon as possible after being made, and certainly within a week if possible—besides, you'll love it so much, it won't linger very long.

As a general rule, ice cream should be transferred to the refrigerator for 20–30 minutes before serving, to let it soften evenly throughout and be perfect to eat.

Scoops

Dip ice cream scoops into ice water just before using—this will make the surface of the ice cream smoother. There are three kinds—one is a basic curved spoon, another a flat paddle used in the gelaterias in Italy, and a third has a lever mechanism operated through the handle. All are good—though I find that an ordinary tablespoon dipped in water works just as well if you don't have a special scoop.

ingredients

As in all cooking, the quality of ingredients will be reflected in the finished results, and none more so than in ice cream making.

Eggs

I use extra-large, free-range, organic eggs. Uncooked or partially cooked eggs should not be served to the very old, the frail, young children, pregnant women, or those with compromised immune systems.

Cream

I always use fresh cream, Italian mascarpone cheese, whole milk, and whole milk yogurt. Using skimmed dairy products compromises flavor and texture—much better to enjoy something special and eat a little less.

Sugar

I use superfine sugar instead of regular sugar, because it has a much finer texture and gives a smoother result. To achieve a deeper flavor in some recipes, I have used light or dark brown sugar. Light adds a delicate toffee flavor: dark will add an intense caramel flavor.

mascarpone ice cream

This lovely, light, milky ice cream—wonderful on its own—is also an excellent base for delicate flavors that can be masked by a rich egg custard.

Put the mascarpone, milk, and sugar in a bowl and beat until thick and smooth. Transfer to an ice cream machine and churn until frozen. Transfer to a freezerproof container and freeze until ready to serve.

Alternatively, to freeze without a machine, see page 8.

8 oz. mascarpone cheese
1 cup whole milk
¾ cup superfine sugar

an ice cream machine (optional)

SERVES 4–6

ice cream

rich vanilla ice cream

Studded with tiny, perfumed seeds, the vanilla bean belongs to the orchid family. Madagascan vanilla is highly regarded and is easily found in gourmet stores, but the finest in the world is believed to be Bourbon. Real vanilla is expensive, but the process that takes it from plant to table is so complex, there is little wonder. Don't be tempted to save money by using cheap, inferior imitation vanilla—the results simply won't be the same. However, do rinse and dry the beans, then bury them deep in a glass jar of sugar to flavor it, ready for your next batch of ice cream.

2 vanilla beans

1¼ cups whole milk

1¼ cups heavy cream

6 extra-large egg yolks

¾ cup superfine sugar

an ice cream machine (optional)

SERVES 4–6

Slit the vanilla beans in half lengthwise and scrape out the seeds with the tip of a sharp knife. Put the beans in a saucepan and the seeds in a bowl.

Pour the milk and cream into the saucepan and bring just to boiling point. Remove from the heat and set aside infuse for at least 30 minutes.

Put the eggs and sugar in a bowl and beat until pale and creamy. Return the cream mixture to the heat and return to a boil. Pour the hot liquid over the eggs, stir until smooth, then pour back into the pan. Reduce the heat and cook over low heat, stirring constantly with a wooden spoon, until the custard has thickened enough to leave a finger trail on the back of the spoon. Take care that the mixture doesn't overheat and scramble.

Let the custard cool completely, then churn in an ice cream machine, transfer to a freezerproof container, and freeze until ready to serve. Alternatively, to freeze without a machine, see page 8.

Note If you have time, the custard will benefit by being left for several hours before churning, to let the flavors develop.

caramel ice cream

Caramel always seems to be high on everyone's list of most loved ice cream flavors, and this is so easy to make, it's sure to become a favorite. Just take care when adding the cold cream to the hot caramel—the mixture can splutter and caramel can cause nasty burns if it touches your skin.

1 cup superfine sugar

2¾ cups heavy cream

⅔ cup whole milk

6 extra-large egg yolks, beaten

a candy thermometer (optional)

a pastry brush

an ice cream machine (optional)

SERVES 4–6

Put the sugar in a heavy saucepan over medium heat and cook until the sugar dissolves completely. Increase the heat and bubble the mixture until it develops a dark amber color—310°F on a candy thermometer. Use a pastry brush dampened with a little water to wash down the sides of the pan and prevent burning.

When the sugar has reached the desired color, carefully pour in the cream. The mixture may spit and seize at this stage. Return the mixture to the heat and stir over low heat until the caramel has dissolved thoroughly in the cream. Let cool.

Heat the milk in a separate saucepan until boiling. Remove from the heat and pour it slowly into the beaten egg, stirring until smooth. Pour the mixture back into the pan and cook over low heat until the mixture thickens to the texture of light cream. Let cool completely, then stir into the caramel mixture. Churn in an ice cream machine, then transfer to a freezerproof container and freeze until ready to serve.

Alternatively, to freeze without a machine, see page 8.

cherry fudge ice cream

It can be a difficult task for a fudge addict like me to make this ice cream without seriously diminishing the required weight of fudge before the time comes to add it to the base mix. What makes this ice cream such a winner, is the generous speckling of chewy fudge and cherries dotted throughout, so I suggest that you do as I have learned to do—play safe and always buy extra to nibble on.

8 oz. mascarpone cheese

1 cup whole milk

¾ cup superfine sugar

8 oz. chocolate fudge, cut into chunks

4 oz. maraschino cherries, chopped, about ½ cup

an ice cream machine (optional)

SERVES 4–6

Put the mascarpone, milk, and sugar in a bowl and beat until smooth. Transfer the mixture to an ice cream machine and churn until almost frozen.

Add the fudge pieces and the chopped cherries and continue churning until the mixture is completely frozen. Transfer to a freezerproof container and freeze until ready to serve.

If you are making the ice cream without a machine, follow the instructions on page 8 and fold in the fudge pieces and chopped cherries before returning the ice cream to the freezer for the final time.

chocolate chip cookie ice cream

Choose good-quality cookies, made with butter if possible—and of course, plenty of real chocolate chips. Cheaper cookies will spoil the ice cream by giving it a greasy aftertaste when frozen.

Put the mascarpone, milk, and sugar in a bowl and beat until smooth. Transfer the mixture to an ice cream machine and churn until almost frozen.

Fold in the crumbled cookies and continue churning until the mixture is completely frozen. Transfer to a freezerproof container and freeze until ready to serve.

If you are making the ice cream without a machine, follow the instructions on page 8 and fold in the crumbled cookies before returning the ice cream to the freezer for the final time.

8 oz. mascarpone cheese

1 cup whole milk

½ cup firmly packed light brown sugar

6 oz. chocolate chip cookies, crumbled

an ice cream machine (optional)

SERVES 4–6

fresh peach ice cream

A perfect sun-ripened peach has to be one of summer's great treats. Firm, yet oozing sweet juices and full of flavor, they make delectable eating—and this is the best time for putting them into ice cream too. In reality, they can vary hugely in flavor, so don't be afraid to adjust the amount of sugar in the recipe to compensate if needed. The mixture should taste slightly over-sweetened before churning, because freezing will reduce the effect of the sugar.

Put the peaches in a food processor, add the mascarpone, milk, sugar, and vodka, if using, and blend to a smooth, thick purée. Churn in an ice cream machine, then transfer to a freezerproof container and freeze until ready to serve.

Alternatively, to freeze without a machine, see page 8.

4 ripe juicy peaches, peeled, halved, and pitted

8 oz. mascarpone cheese

¾ cup whole milk

1 cup superfine sugar

3 tablespoons vodka (optional)

an ice cream machine (optional)

SERVES 4–6

new york cheesecake ice cream

All the flavors of a luscious, lemony New York cheesecake, right down to the crunch of the cookie base. Don't be tempted to use low-fat cream cheese—the flavor and texture won't be the same. Just eat, enjoy, and power-walk to work tomorrow!

Pour the milk and cream into a saucepan and heat to boiling point.

Put the eggs and sugar in a bowl and beat until pale and creamy. Pour the hot liquid over the eggs, stir until smooth, then pour back into the saucepan. Reduce the heat and cook over low heat, stirring constantly with a wooden spoon, until the custard has thickened enough to leave a finger trail on the back of the spoon. Take care that the mixture doesn't overheat and scramble.

Remove from the heat and let cool completely. Beat in the cream cheese, lemon juice, and zest until smooth. Churn in an ice cream machine until almost frozen. Add the crumbled cookies and continue to churn until the mixture is completely frozen. Transfer to a freezerproof container and freeze until ready to serve.

If you are making the ice cream without a machine, follow the instructions on page 8 and fold in the crumbled cookies before returning the ice cream to the freezer for the final time.

½ cup whole milk

½ cup heavy cream

4 extra-large egg yolks

¾ cup superfine sugar

10 oz. cream cheese

grated zest and freshly squeezed juice of 2 unwaxed lemons

4 oz. oatmeal cookies, crumbled into small pieces

an ice cream machine (optional)

SERVES 4–6

buttered pecan and maple syrup ice cream

Toasting the pecans in butter gives them delicious flavor, but don't let yourself be distracted during the process—sizzling nuts wait for no man (or woman!)

2 tablespoons unsalted butter

6 oz. pecans, coarsely chopped, about 1½ cups

1¼ cups whole milk

1¼ cups heavy cream

6 extra-large egg yolks

½ cup firmly packed light brown sugar

⅔ cup maple syrup

an ice cream machine (optional)

SERVES 4–6

Melt the butter in a heavy saucepan, add the pecans, and sauté gently over low heat until golden and fragrant. Remove to a plate and let cool.

Pour the milk and cream into a separate saucepan and bring to a boil. Put the egg yolks and sugar in a bowl and beat until smooth. Pour the hot liquid over the eggs, stir until smooth, then return to the saucepan. Reduce the heat and cook over low heat, stirring constantly, until the custard has thickened, taking care not to let the mixture overheat and scramble. Add the maple syrup and let cool completely.

Churn in an ice cream machine until almost frozen. Add the chopped pecans and continue to churn until the mixture is completely frozen. Transfer to a freezerproof container and freeze until ready to serve.

If you are making the ice cream without a machine, follow the instructions on page 8 and fold in the pecans just before returning the ice cream to the freezer for the final time.

dark chocolate mint crackle ice cream

I'm sometimes asked how I judge the amount of each ingredient to start with when I develop recipes from scratch. Here, it happened by chance. Trying to recreate the flavor of my favorite crackly after-dinner mints in an ice cream, I started with two 3½-oz. bars of very tempting bittersweet chocolate. Then I ate two squares. By a stroke of luck, I was left with the perfect quantity to produce this deliciously different ice cream.

7 oz. bittersweet chocolate, minus 2 squares

½ cup superfine sugar

3 tablespoons crème de cacao (optional but delicious)

3–4 tablespoons light brown sugar

a small bunch of fresh mint, finely chopped

an ice cream machine (optional)

SERVES 4–6

Melt the chocolate, sugar, and ¾ cup water in a heatproof bowl set over a saucepan of simmering water, or microwave on HIGH for 1 minute. Add the crème de cacao, if using, then let cool completely. Churn in an ice cream machine until almost frozen. Add the brown sugar and chopped mint and continue to churn until the mixture is completely frozen. Transfer to a freezerproof container and freeze until ready to serve.

If you are making the ice cream without a machine, follow the instructions on page 8 and fold in the brown sugar and mint just before returning the ice cream to the freezer for the final time.

peanut brittle ice cream

Rather than raw peanuts in their skins, use roasted, lightly salted peanuts. The small amount of salt on the nuts seems to enhance the flavor. Keep a couple of tablespoons of the brittle to sprinkle over the ice cream when serving.

1¼ cups whole milk

1¼ cups heavy cream

6 extra-large egg yolks

¾ cup superfine sugar

peanut brittle

¾ cup superfine sugar

1 cup peanuts (see recipe introduction)

a pastry brush

a candy thermometer (optional)

a baking sheet, lightly buttered

an ice cream machine (optional)

SERVES 4–6

Put the sugar and ½ cup water in a heavy saucepan over low heat and cook until the sugar has completely dissolved. Use a pastry brush dampened with a little water to wash down the sides of the pan and prevent burning.

Increase the heat and bubble the mixture until it develops a dark amber color—310°F on a candy thermometer. Stir in the peanuts, then immediately pour the mixture onto the prepared baking sheet. Let cool completely, then break into small pieces.

Pour the milk and cream into a saucepan and heat to boiling point.

Put the eggs and sugar in a bowl and beat until smooth. Pour the hot liquid over the eggs, stir until smooth, then return the mixture to the saucepan. Reduce the heat and cook over low heat, stirring constantly with a wooden spoon, until the custard has thickened enough to leave a finger trail on the back of the spoon. Take care that the mixture doesn't overheat and scramble.

Let the custard cool completely. Churn in an ice cream machine until almost frozen. Add the broken peanut brittle and continue to churn until the mixture is completely frozen. Transfer to a freezerproof container and freeze until ready to serve.

If you are making the ice cream without a machine, follow the instructions on page 8 and fold in the crushed peanut brittle just before returning the ice cream to the freezer for the final time.

sherry and raisin ice cream

On a trip to Spain's sherry-making region several years ago, I fell in love with the gloriously rich, raisiny sherry called Pedro Ximénez. I've used it to make this addictive ice cream ever since, although any sweet, syrupy sherry or an Italian Marsala would make a suitable alternative. For a special touch, soak a few extra raisins to serve with the ice cream.

Put the raisins in a bowl and pour over the sherry. Set aside for as long as possible to plump up and flavor the raisins.

Put the mascarpone, milk, and sugar in a bowl and beat until thick and smooth. Churn in an ice cream machine until the ice cream is almost frozen. Add the soaked raisins and sherry and continue churning until the mixture is completely frozen. Transfer to a freezerproof container and freeze until ready to serve.

If you are making the ice cream without a machine, follow the instructions on page 8 and fold in the raisins and sherry just before returning the ice cream to the freezer for the final time.

⅔ **cup raisins**

½ **cup sweet sherry, such as Pedro Ximénez**

8 **oz. mascarpone cheese**

1 **cup whole milk**

¾ **cup superfine sugar**

an ice cream machine (optional)

SERVES 4–6

licorice ice cream

I always justify a second portion of this unusual ice cream by reminding myself that licorice contains a good dose of vitamin E, plus B vitamins and valuable trace elements. It tastes fantastic too.

6 oz. black licorice, chopped into small pieces

2¾ cups heavy cream

1–2 whole star anise

½ cup firmly packed light brown sugar

4 extra-large egg yolks, beaten

1¼ cups whole milk

an ice cream machine (optional)

SERVES 6

Put the licorice pieces in a saucepan, add the cream and star anise, and heat gently until the licorice has almost dissolved. Transfer to a food processor, add the sugar, and blend until smooth.

Put the egg yolks and milk in a clean saucepan and stir over low heat until the mixture has thickened. Add it to the mixture in the processor and blend again.

Let the mixture cool completely. Churn in an ice cream machine until frozen, then transfer to a freezerproof container and freeze until ready to serve.

If you are making the ice cream without a machine, follow the instructions on page 8.

peppermint ice cream

Minty and crunchy, this is a must-try ice cream for all peppermint fans. It's another favorite in my house—but please don't breathe a word to my dentist.

Put the mascarpone, milk, and sugar in a bowl and beat until thick and smooth. Churn in an ice cream machine until the mixture is almost frozen and then add the crushed humbugs. Continue churning until completely frozen. Transfer to a freezerproof container and freeze until ready to serve.

If you are making the ice cream without a machine, follow the instructions on page 8 and fold in the crushed peppermints just before returning the ice cream to the freezer for the final time.

8 oz. mascarpone cheese

1 cup whole milk

¾ cup superfine sugar

6 oz. peppermints or candycanes, coarsely crushed

an ice cream machine (optional)

SERVES 6

pineapple and fresh mint ice cream

Pineapple and custard have always made a great match—especially when the custard is rich, eggy, and infused with real vanilla. Alternatively, omit the vanilla and substitute a little fresh mint, and the combination is utterly sublime too. Use a good, ripe, fragrant pineapple—the flesh of an under-ripe pineapple will be sinewy when blended and give the ice cream a stringy, grainy texture.

1 large, ripe pineapple

8 oz. mascarpone cheese

3 tablespoons Malibu liqueur or white rum

¾ cup whole milk

4 extra-large egg yolks

¾ cup superfine sugar

a small bunch of mint, finely chopped

an ice cream machine (optional)

SERVES 4–6

Peel the pineapple and cut out the core. Chop the flesh and put in a food processor or blender. Add the mascarpone and Malibu and blend until smooth. Set aside.

Heat the milk in a saucepan until it reaches the boiling point. Put the eggs and sugar in a bowl and beat until pale and creamy. Pour the hot milk over the eggs and stir until smooth, then return to the stove and cook over low heat, stirring constantly, until the custard has thickened, taking care not to let it overheat and scramble.

Let the custard cool completely, then add to the puréed pineapple mixture. Add the chopped mint and mix well. Churn in an ice cream machine until frozen, then transfer to a freezerproof container and freeze until ready to serve.

If you are making the ice cream without a machine, follow the instructions on page 8.

malibu and coconut ice cream

This is a creamy dream of an ice cream—it isn't churned in a machine, but has a lovely light texture provided by whipped egg whites—reminiscent of Italian semifreddo. Serve it in scoops, or make in a loaf pan or terrine mold and cut it into slices to serve with wafer-thin slices of fresh pineapple.

3 extra-large egg whites

¾ cup superfine sugar

¾ cup coconut milk

8 oz. mascarpone cheese

3 tablespoons Malibu liqueur or white rum

SERVES 4–6

Put the egg whites and sugar in a bowl and beat until stiff and glossy. Put the coconut milk, mascarpone, Malibu, and ⅓ cup water in a bowl and beat until smooth. Carefully but thoroughly fold in the egg white mixture. Transfer to a freezerproof container and freeze overnight.

southern comfort, saffron, and ginger ice cream

Orange-blossom honey works particularly well in this gorgeous, saffron-scented ice cream, but if you have difficulty finding it, use any clear, light, flowery honey instead—a strong-tasting honey will drown the delicate balance of flavors.

1¼ cups milk

a good pinch of saffron threads

4 extra-large egg yolks

¾ cup superfine sugar

¼ cup orange blossom honey or clover honey

¼ cup Southern Comfort

1 cup mascarpone cheese

4 oz. crystallized ginger, coarsely chopped, about ¾ cup

an ice cream machine (optional)

SERVES 6

Pour the milk into a saucepan and add the saffron threads. Bring to the boil, turn off the heat, and leave to infuse for at least 30 minutes.

Put the egg yolks and sugar in a bowl and beat until light and creamy. Return the milk to a boil and pour it over the egg mixture, stirring until smooth. Return the custard to the stove and cook over low heat, stirring constantly, until it has thickened, taking care not to let the mixture overheat. Stir in the honey and Southern Comfort.

Let cool completely, then beat in the mascarpone until thoroughly blended and smooth. Churn in an ice cream machine until almost frozen, then fold in the crystallized ginger. Continue to churn until the mixture is completely frozen, then transfer to a freezerproof container and freeze until ready to serve.

If you are making the ice cream without a machine, follow the instructions on page 8 and fold in the ginger just before returning the ice cream to the freezer for the final time.

easy apricot ice cream

This is such an easy ice cream to make. I always feel as if I'm cheating, but in reality, the season for good, sweet apricots is so short that this ice cream gives a consistently better flavor—you can have a little taste of summer every month of the year. The quality of the conserve is crucial to the recipe's success; always check the label and choose a first-rate conserve with at least 2 oz. of fruit in every 3½ oz. of jam.

8 oz. mascarpone cheese

¾ cup whole milk

½ cup superfine sugar

8 oz. apricot conserve

an ice cream machine (optional)

SERVES 4–6

Put the mascarpone, milk, sugar, and 7 oz. of the conserve in a bowl and beat until thick and smooth. Churn in an ice cream machine until almost frozen, then fold in the remaining apricot conserve to give a ripple effect. Continue churning until completely frozen, then transfer to a freezerproof container and freeze until ready to serve.

If you are making the ice cream without a machine, follow the instructions on page 8 and fold in the remaining apricot conserve just before returning the ice cream to the freezer for the final time.

blueberry streusel ice cream

Delicious and crunchy, streusel means "sprinkle" in German—it is a crumbly topping made of flour, sugar, butter, and spices. I use dried blueberries in this ice cream rather than fresh, because they plump up so nicely when soaked in the vodka. They give a lovely chewy texture and contrast beautifully with the crisp streusel.

Put the blueberries in a small bowl, sprinkle with vodka, and set aside to soak.

To make the streusel, preheat the oven to 350°F. Put the butter, flour, and sugar in a bowl and rub with your fingertips until the butter is evenly incorporated and the mixture forms chunky crumbs. Add the walnuts and spread the mixture in an even layer on a baking sheet. Bake for 10–15 minutes, until crisp and golden, then remove from the oven and let cool completely.

Put the mascarpone, milk, and sugar in a bowl and whisk until thick and creamy. Churn in an ice cream machine until the ice cream is almost totally frozen. Add the blueberries, vodka, and the streusel chunks, and continue churning until the mixture is completely frozen. Transfer to a freezerproof container and freeze until ready to serve.

If you are making the ice cream without a machine, follow the instructions on page 8 and fold in the blueberries, vodka, and streusel crumbs just before returning the ice cream to the freezer for the final time.

⅔ cup dried blueberries

3 tablespoons vodka

8 oz. mascarpone cheese

1 cup whole milk

½ cup superfine sugar

streusel

7 tablespoons unsalted butter

1 cup all-purpose flour

½ cup firmly packed light brown sugar

2 tablespoons chopped walnuts

a baking sheet

an ice cream machine (optional)

SERVES 4–6

lemon yogurt ice cream

A light, zingy yogurt-based ice cream is lovely to serve with ripe summer berries, but my son Tim loves it served in a cone. Do choose a good-quality, creamy, full-fat yogurt, or the ice cream will be far too acidic and the texture too icy.

2 cups full-fat plain yogurt

grated zest and freshly squeezed juice of 2 unwaxed lemons

½ cup superfine sugar

an ice cream machine (optional)

SERVES 4–6

Put the yogurt, lemon zest and juice, and sugar in a bowl and stir until smooth. Churn in an ice cream machine, then transfer to a freezerproof container and freeze until ready to serve.

Alternatively, to freeze without a machine, see page 8.

frozen yogurts, sorbets, and slushes

mango, mint, and lime frozen yogurt

This makes a fabulous finish to spicy Asian and Indian meals.

Peel the mango and cut the flesh away from the pit. Put the flesh in a food processor, add the sugar, yogurt, lime juice, and mint leaves and blend until smooth. Churn in an ice cream machine until frozen. Transfer to a freezerproof container and freeze until ready to serve.

Alternatively, to freeze without a machine, see page 8.

1 large, very ripe mango

½ cup superfine sugar

2 cups whole milk plain yogurt

freshly squeezed juice of 1 large lime

a small handful of mint leaves, finely chopped

an ice cream machine (optional)

SERVES 4–6

summer berry frozen yogurt

Use good, creamy, plain yogurt for this recipe and you will be rewarded with a delectable ice cream. A tart, low-fat yogurt will give a sour, acidic flavor and an unpleasant, icy texture. Frozen fruit works well in this recipe too.

1 lb. mixed summer berries, such as strawberries, blackberries, and raspberries

¾ cup superfine sugar

16 oz. whole milk plain yogurt

an ice cream machine (optional)

SERVES 4

Warm the berries and sugar in a saucepan over low heat for several minutes, until the fruit begins to release its juices. Transfer to a food processor and blend to a purée. Push the purée through a fine-meshed nylon sieve to remove the seeds. Stir in the yogurt.

Churn in an ice cream machine until frozen. Transfer to a freezerproof container and freeze until ready to serve.

Alternatively, to freeze without a machine, see page 8.

mojito slush

1 cup superfine sugar

a generous bunch of mint leaves, very finely chopped, plus extra to serve

½ cup Bacardi or other white rum

freshly squeezed juice of 4 limes

½ cup sparkling water

an ice cream machine (optional)

SERVES 4

A mojito is a wonderful cocktail made with white rum, fresh mint, and lime. Frozen to a smooth, zingy slush, it makes a gorgeous light ice to serve as dessert, or to enjoy outside on a hot sunny day. I usually substitute Malibu for the customary white rum; the subtle hint of coconut adds a special touch. Take care though—it's so addictive, you can get sozzled on an ice like this.

Put the sugar and ¾ cup water in a saucepan and heat until the sugar has completely dissolved. Let the mixture bubble for 1–2 minutes until slightly syrupy. Remove from the heat, stir in the mint, and leave to infuse until cold.

Strain the mixture to remove the mint and stir in the Bacardi, lime juice, and sparkling water. Churn in an ice cream machine until frozen, then transfer to a freezerproof container and freeze until ready to serve.

Alternatively, to freeze without a machine, see page 8.

vodka, fizz, and lemon slush
(lemon colonello)

This is my version of an amazing cocktail-style slush that I tasted with good friends at a lovely beachside restaurant in southern Spain. After a stunning fish-laden paella, we slurped our way through a couple of these lip-smacking concoctions. We were convinced the recipe came special delivery, direct from heaven. I'm not sure what method of divine intervention helped it reach Los Sardinales, but we were over the moon about being there to intercept it.

½ cup vodka

1¾ cups sparkling wine,
such as prosecco
or cava

8 scoops lemon sorbet
(see below)

⅔ cup heavy cream

lemon sorbet

1 cup superfine sugar

4 juicy, unwaxed lemons

*an ice cream machine
(optional)*

Serves 4

To make the sorbet, put the sugar in a saucepan with ¾ cup water. Heat until the sugar has completely disscolved, then let the mixture bubble for 1–2 minutes until slightly syrupy. Remove from the heat, add the grated zest from 2 of the lemons, and the juice from all of them. You should be aiming for about ½ cup of lemon juice.

Leave the mixture until completely cold, then churn in an ice cream machine until frozen. Transfer to the freezer until ready to serve. If you are making the ice cream without a machine, follow the instructions on page 8.

To make the slush, put the vodka, wine, lemon sorbet, and cream in a food processor and blend well. Churn in an ice cream machine until slushy, then serve immediately.

Alternatively, to freeze without a machine, see page 8.

frozen treats

cranberry and orange frozen treats

Cranberry and orange juices make a fabulous fruity combination, as any devotee of Sea Breeze will attest. Delicious!

2¾ cups cranberry juice

¾ cup freshly squeezed orange juice

1 cup superfine sugar

frozen treat molds

MAKES ABOUT 10

Pour the cranberry and orange juices into a bowl, add the sugar, and stir until the sugar has completely dissolved. Pour into frozen treat molds and transfer to the freezer until frozen.

yellow grapefruit frozen treats

2¾ cups yellow grapefruit juice (about 6 juicy grapefruits)

1 cup superfine sugar

frozen treat molds

MAKES ABOUT 10

Use yellow or pink grapefruit to make these delicious, thirst-quenching frozen treats—popular with all ages. All that vitamin C has to be a bonus too.

Put the grapefruit juice, sugar, and ¾ cup water in a bowl and stir until the sugar has completely dissolved. Pour into the frozen treat molds and transfer to the freezer until frozen.

ice cream ice cubes for sodas

Drop these ice cream ice cubes into tall glasses of lemonade or other soda—to create old-fashioned ice cream sodas. Try topping up real fruit cordials with sparkling water and adding a few cubes— blackcurrant cordial is especially nice. They're also wonderful in sparkling fruit drinks, smoothies, and milk shakes.

8 oz. mascarpone cheese

1½ cups whole milk

¾ cup superfine sugar

MAKES 18–24,
depending on size of tray used

Put the mascarpone, milk, and sugar in a bowl and beat until thick and smooth. Transfer the mixture to ice cube trays and freeze until solid.

sauces

fresh berry sauce

This gorgeous raspberry sauce is sublime with vanilla or mascarpone ice cream. The method used to make it can be applied to most fresh summer or fall berries; strawberries, blackberries, and loganberries all work beautifully. Just adjust the sugar to taste.

8 oz. fresh ripe raspberries
2 tablespoons Framboise or Cointreau liqueur
¼ cup sugar

SERVES 6–8

Put the raspberries in a blender or food processor and purée until smooth. Push the mixture through a fine-meshed nylon sieve to remove the seeds. If your sieve is large and sturdy, you can omit the blender by pushing the berries directly though the sieve with the back of a wooden spoon.

Add the liqueur and sweeten the purée with the sugar. The exact amount of sugar will vary according to the ripeness of the fruit.

orange and grand marnier sauce

This is glossy and gorgeous.

3 tablespoons superfine sugar
grated zest and freshly squeezed juice of 2 large, unwaxed oranges
¼ cup Grand Marnier
2 tablespoons concentrated orange juice

SERVES 4

Put the sugar in a saucepan over low heat and stir until the sugar has melted. Add the orange zest, then the Grand Marnier. Carefully light the Grand Marnier with a long match. When the flames die down, add the orange juice. Bubble lightly over low heat for a few minutes until the sauce reduces and thickens slightly.

hot jamaican rum butter sauce

Pour this delicious sauce over the mascarpone ice cream (page 10) and add a little ground spice to complement the ice cream's intended partner. Stir in a pinch or two of finely ground star anise, or a tiny sprinkle of nutmeg or cinnamon.

⅓ cup dark rum
½ cup firmly packed dark brown sugar
7 tablespoons unsalted butter

SERVES 6–8

Put the rum, sugar, and butter in a heavy saucepan and stir until the sugar has completely dissolved. Serve hot.

caramel sauce

This popular sauce will complement many of the ice creams in this book. As with the caramel ice cream, take care when adding the cream to the hot caramel.

1 cup sugar
2 tablespoons light corn syrup
1¼ cups heavy cream

a candy thermometer (optional)

SERVES 6–8

Put the sugar and corn syrup in a heavy saucepan over gentle heat and stir until the sugar has completely dissolved. Increase the heat and cook until the mixture turns a dark golden amber color—310°F on a candy thermometer. Remove from the heat and carefully stir in the cream, taking care, as the mixture will splutter.

Stir until the caramel has dissolved into the cream. Serve hot or cold.

chocolate sauce

This is a rich sauce for lovers of bittersweet chocolate. For a lighter, sweeter alternative, replace the water with heavy cream.

4 oz. bittersweet chocolate
2 tablespoons light corn syrup

SERVES 4

Put the chocolate, corn syrup, and ¼ cup water in a heatproof bowl set over a saucepan of gently simmering water (or microwave on HIGH for 1 minute) and stir until smooth. Serve hot or cold.

butterscotch praline sauce

Crunchy macadamia praline turns an already wonderful toffee sauce into something special. To vary the flavor, try ringing the changes by using different varieties of nuts. I like toasted hazelnuts, and walnuts are wonderful too.

praline

½ cup superfine sugar

⅔ cup macadamia nuts

sauce

⅔ cup superfine sugar

2 tablespoons light corn syrup

1¼ cups heavy cream

freshly grated nutmeg, to serve

a baking sheet, lightly buttered

a pastry brush

a candy thermometer (optional)

SERVES 6–8

Put the sugar and ⅓ cup water in a heavy saucepan over low heat and cook until the sugar has completely dissolved. Use a pastry brush dampened with a little water to wash down the sides of the pan and prevent burning.

Increase the heat and bubble the mixture until it develops a dark amber color—310°F on a candy thermometer. Stir in the macadamia nuts and immediately spoon the mixture onto the prepared sheet. Let cool completely, then break into small pieces.

To make the sauce, put the sugar and corn syrup in a heavy saucepan over gentle heat and stir until the sugar has completely dissolved. Increase the heat and cook until the mixture turns a dark golden amber color—310°F on a candy thermometer.

Remove from the heat and carefully stir in the cream until the caramel has dissolved and the sauce is smooth. Stir in the praline. Serve hot or cold with nutmeg on top.

index

conversion charts

Weights and measures have been rounded up or down slightly to make measuring easier.

Volume equivalents:

American	Metric	Imperial
1 teaspoon	5 ml	
1 tablespoon	15 ml	
¼ cup	60 ml	2 fl.oz.
⅓ cup	75 ml	2½ fl.oz.
½ cup	125 ml	4 fl.oz.
⅔ cup	150 ml	5 fl.oz. (¼ pint)
¾ cup	175 ml	6 fl.oz.
1 cup	250 ml	8 fl.oz.

Weight equivalents:

Imperial	Metric
1 oz.	25 g
2 oz.	50 g
3 oz.	75 g
4 oz.	125 g
5 oz.	150 g
6 oz.	175 g
7 oz.	200 g
8 oz. (½ lb.)	250 g
9 oz.	275 g
10 oz.	300 g
11 oz.	325 g
12 oz.	375 g
13 oz.	400 g
14 oz.	425 g
15 oz.	475 g
16 oz. (1 lb.)	500 g
2 1b.	1 kg

Measurements:

Inches	Cm
¼ inch	5 mm
½ inch	1 cm
¾ inch	1.5 cm
1 inch	2.5 cm
2 inches	5 cm
3 inches	7 cm
4 inches	10 cm
5 inches	12 cm
6 inches	15 cm
7 inches	18 cm
8 inches	20 cm
9 inches	23 cm
10 inches	25 cm
11 inches	28 cm
12 inches	30 cm

Oven temperatures:

110°C	(225°F)	Gas ¼
120°C	(250°F)	Gas ½
140°C	(275°F)	Gas 1
150°C	(300°F)	Gas 2
160°C	(325°F)	Gas 3
180°C	(350°F)	Gas 4
190°C	(375°F)	Gas 5
200°C	(400°F)	Gas 6
220°C	(425°F)	Gas 7
230°C	(450°F)	Gas 8
240°C	(475°F)	Gas 9